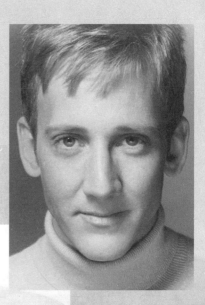

A V A L O N · J O Y

ISBN 0-634-02151-6

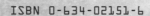

HAL·LEONARD®
CORPORATION
7777 W. BLUEMOUND RD. P.O. BOX 13819 MILWAUKEE, WI 53213

Visit Hal Leonard Online at
www.halleonard.com

JOY (TO THE WORLD)

Words and Music by DAN MUCKALA,
GRANT CUNNINGHAM and BROWN BANNISTER

D.S. al Coda

ANGELS MEDLEY

Arranged by TIM AKERS, CHARLIE PEACOCK,
MICHAEL PASSONS, JANNA POTTER,
NIKKI HASSMAN and JODY McBRAYER

14

DON'T SAVE IT ALL
FOR CHRISTMAS DAY

Words and Music by CELINE DION,
PETER ZIZZO and RIC WAKE

Don't get so bus-y that you miss

* Key of recording: Db

JESUS BORN ON THIS DAY

Words and Music by MARIAH CAREY
and WALTER AFANASIEFF

*Vocal harmony 2nd time only

WINTER WONDERLAND

Words by DICK SMITH
Music by FELIX BERNARD

40

LIGHT A CANDLE

Words and Music by JOEL LINDSAY
and WAYNE HAUN

Slowly

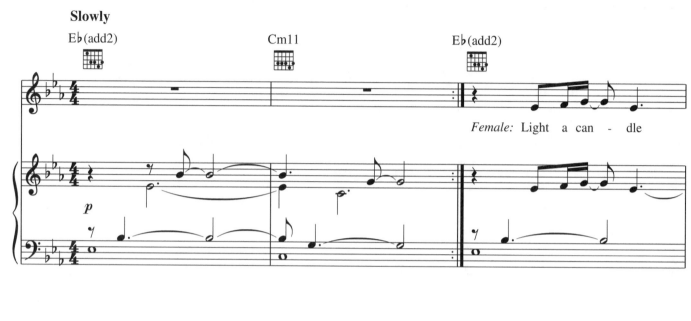

Female: Light a can - dle

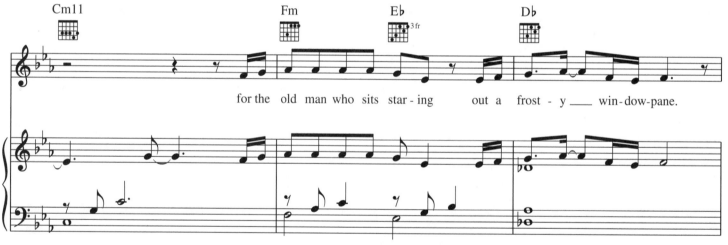

for the old man who sits star - ing out a frost - y ___ win-dow-pane.

Light a can - dle ___ for the wom-an who is lone - ly and ev-'ry

50

GOOD NEWS

Words and Music by
ROB MATHES

Original key: Ab major. This edition has been transposed down one half-step to be more playable.

THE CHRISTMAS SONG
(Chestnuts Roasting on an Open Fire)

Music and Lyric by MEL TORME
and ROBERT WELLS

66

70

MANGER MEDLEY

Arranged by MICHAEL PASSONS,
JODY McBRAYER, JANNA POTTER,
CHERIE PALIOTTA and ROGER RYAN

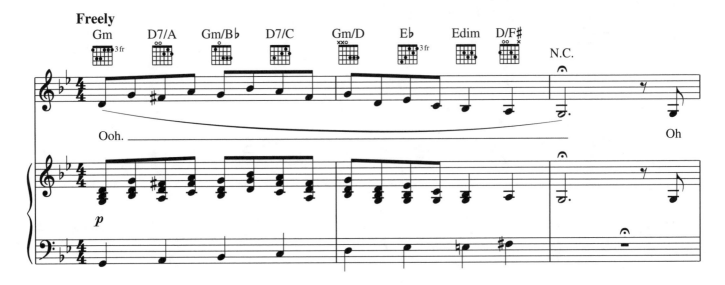

Slower

WE ARE THE REASON

Words and Music by
DAVID MEECE

84